A PRIMARY SOURCE
LIBRARY OF
AMERICAN CITIZENSHIP ™

The Constitution

Josepha Sherman

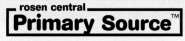

rosen central
Primary Source™

The Rosen Publishing Group, Inc., New York

Published in 2004 by The Rosen Publishing Group, Inc.
29 East 21st Street, New York, NY 10010

Library of Congress Cataloging-in-Publication Data

Sherman, Josepha.
The Constitution/Josepha Sherman.—1st ed.
    v. cm.—(A primary source library of American citizenship)
Includes bibliographical references and index.
Contents: The start of a new country—The Constitutional Convention—The United States Constitution.
ISBN 0-8239-4473-5 (library binding)
1. Constitutional history—United States—Juvenile literature. [1. Constitutional law—United States. 2. Constitutional history—United States. 3. United States. Constitutional Convention (1787)] I. Title. II. Series.
KF4520.Z9S52 2004
342.73'029—dc21

                                                                                2003007259

Manufactured in the United States of America

On the cover: At lower left, George Washington presides at the Constitutional Convention as the delegates sign the Constitution. At upper right, Independence Hall in Philadelphia, where the signing took place.

Cover (background), pp. 9, 15, 21 © Records of the Continental and Confederation Congresses and the Constitutional Convention, 1174-1789, Record Group 360, National Archives; cover (top right), p. 4 © Historical Picture Archive/Corbis; cover (bottom left), pp. 12, 19 23 © Library of Congress, Prints and Photographs Division; p. 5 © Lester Lefkowitz/Corbis; p. 6 © Print Collection, Miriam and Ira D. Wallach Division of Art, Prints and Photographs, the New York Public Library, Astor, Lenox, and Tilden Foundations; pp. 7, 8, 14, 16, 24, 26 © Hulton/Archive/Getty Images; p. 10 © National Portrait Gallery, Smithsonian Institution/Art Resource, NY; pp. 11, 13 © Library of Congress, Manuscript Division; p. 17 © Independence National Historical Park; pp. 18, 25 courtesy of *The American Revolution: A Picture Source Book,* Dover Pictorial Archive Series; p. 20 © Library of Congress, Rare Book and Special Collections Division; pp. 27, 28, 29 (top and bottom) © General Records of the United States Government, Record Group 11, National Archives; p. 30 © Library of Congress, Geography and Map Division.

Designer: Tahara Hasan

Contents

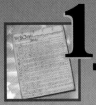

1 The Start of a New Country

The day was May 25, 1787. The place was the Pennsylvania State House in the city of Philadelphia. People passing by the building must have wondered what was going on. Dirt had been shoveled over the cobblestones that paved the streets to silence the sounds of horses and carriages. Guards stood at the doors. What was happening?

This is how the Pennsylvania State House, now Independence Hall, appeared at the time of the debate on the Constitution.

The assembly room of the Pennsylvania State House, where the delegates of the Constitutional Convention met. Restored to its original appearance, the room is now open to the public.

Inside the state house, 55 men were meeting for the Constitutional Convention. These men had waged a war against England for American independence. The war had ended in 1781, with the Americans victorious. The thirteen colonies, now states, that these men represented were too small to survive as separate countries. They had formed one nation under the Articles of Confederation.

Engraver Amos Doolittle created this scene depicting the retreat to Boston of British troops after the skirmishes at Lexington and Concord, the first battles of the Revolutionary War.

THE UNITED STATES
After the Treaty of 1783

Showing the claims of the older States
to the Western Lands

The Territory of the Thirteen Original States
after claims had been ceded is tinted.

The Claims to the Western Lands are shown
in border tint of the same color as
the claiming State.

States having no claims are colored thus:

English Statute Miles

This map of the United States shows the thirteen states that existed after the Treaty of Paris ended the Revolutionary War in 1783. Also shown are the western territories of the Ohio Valley claimed by those states.

The Articles of Confederation were an agreement to create a central, or federal, government. The people gave their new, united country the name of the United States of America. But the Articles of Confederation had not made the central government strong enough. Now the 55 delegates had come to Philadelphia to make up a new set of rules, a constitution, for the United States. There was much work to do, and they needed to think clearly, without people interrupting or making noise.

A portrait of Roger Sherman (1721–1793), the only American to sign the Declaration of Independence, the Articles of Confederation, and the Constitution of the United States.

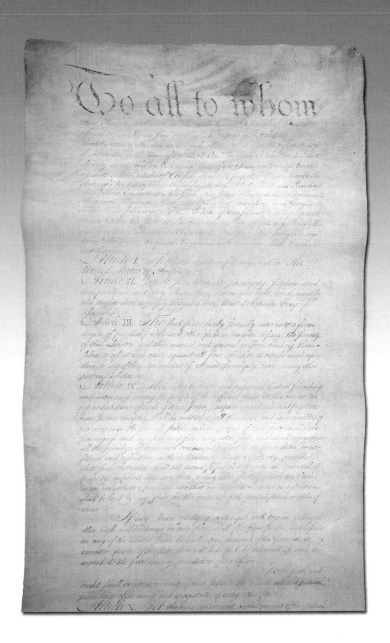

The Articles of Confederation, adopted in 1777. The government it created proved too weak to survive, and this document was replaced by the Constitution.

2 The Constitutional Convention

General George Washington from Virginia was selected to be the head of the Constitutional Convention. That was the last thing on which everyone agreed for days. The 55 delegates argued all through the summer, writing and rewriting parts of the new Constitution. It was hot that summer, and the men must have been miserable. But they kept working.

This unfinished portrait of George Washington (1732–1799), the first president of the United States, was painted by the artist Gilbert Stuart (1755–1828).

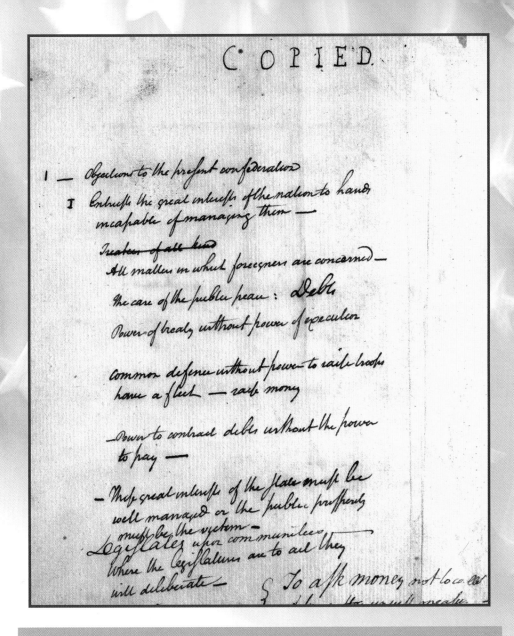

Alexander Hamilton wrote these notes for a speech he gave at the Constitutional Convention. Hamilton supported the establishment of a strong central government and advocated for limitations on the rights of individual states.

The delegates had to decide how much power the central government should have, how representatives from each state should be elected, and how many of those representatives should come from each state. Delegates from the more populous states wanted more representatives. Delegates from the less populous states argued that this was unfair.

George Washington addresses the delegates at the Constitutional Convention in 1787.

A C T S

PASSED AT A

C O N G R E S S

OF THE

UNITED STATES

OF

A M E R I C A,

BEGUN AND HELD AT THE CITY OF NEW-
YORK, ON *WEDNESDAY* THE *FOURTH*
OF *MARCH*, IN THE YEAR
M.DCC.LXXXIX.
AND OF THE
INDEPENDENCE OF THE *UNITED STATES*,
THE THIRTEENTH.

Being the Acts passed at the First Session of the First Congress
of the United States, to wit, New-Hampshire, Massachusetts,
Connecticut, New-York, New-Jersey, Pennsylvania, Dela-
ware, Maryland, Virginia, South-Carolina, and Georgia;
which Eleven States respectively ratified the Constitution of Government for the United States, proposed
by the Federal Convention, held in Philadelphia,
on the Seventeenth of September, One Thou-
sand Seven Hundred and Eighty-Seven.

N E W - Y O R K:

Printed by HODGE, ALLEN and CAMPBELL,
and sold at their respective Book-Stores;
Also, by T. LLOYD.

M.DCC.LXXXIX.

Signed by President Washington, this early act of Congress in 1789 added to the Constitution the amendments that would come to be called the Bill of Rights.

The more populous states liked what was called the Virginia Plan. This said that the more people in a state, the more representatives. The less populous states liked the New Jersey Plan. This said that all states should have equal numbers of representatives. There were so many fights about which plan should be chosen that the convention nearly broke up.

Continental soldier and politician Charles C. Pinckney fought at the Battles of Brandywine and Germantown and rose to the rank of major general. He helped frame the Constitution and ran for the presidency twice.

State of the resolutions submitted to the consideration of the House by the honorable Mr. Randolph, as altered, amended, and agreed to in a committee of the whole House.

1 Resolved that it is the opinion of this Committee that a national government ought to be established consisting of a Supreme Legislature, Judiciary, and Executive.

2 Resolved that the national Legislature ought to consist of Two Branches.

3 Resolved that the members of the first branch of the national Legislature ought to be elected by the People of the several States for the term of Three years. to receive fixed Stipends, by which they may be compensated for the devotion of their time to public service to be paid out of the national Treasury. to be ineligible to any Office established by a particular State or under the authority of the United States (except those peculiarly belonging to the functions of the first branch) during the term of service, and under the national government for the space of one year after its expiration.

4 Resolved. that the members of the second Branch of the national Legislature ought to be chosen by the individual Legislatures. to be of the age of thirty years at least. to hold their offices for a term sufficient to ensure their independency, namely Seven years. to receive fixed Stipends, by which they may be compensated for the devotion of their time to public service — to be paid out of the national Treasury. to be ineligible to any office established by a particular State, or under the authority of the United States (except those peculiarly belonging to the functions of the second branch) during the term of service, and under the national government, for the space of one year after its expiration.

The original draft of the Virginia Plan was devised by Virginia delegates James Madison and Edmund Randolph at the Constitutional Convention. The plan established two houses of government, the Senate and the House of Representatives.

At last the delegates from Connecticut came up with a compromise. There would be two houses of government, the House of Representatives and the Senate. Representatives to the House would be elected in proportion to the number of people in each state. In the Senate, the same number of senators would come from each state. Everyone at the meeting finally agreed on this compromise. It became known as the Great Compromise.

Alexander Hamilton was a soldier in the Continental army, a delegate to both the Continental Congress and the Constitutional Convention, an author of the Federalist Papers, and the secretary of the treasury.

Oliver Ellsworth, a Connecticut delegate to the Constitutional
Convention, helped devise the compromise that created a separate
Senate and House of Representatives. Washington later appointed
him a justice of the Supreme Court.

3 The United States Constitution

Delegates to the Constitutional Convention knew what it was like to live under the rule of the king of England. The king made all the rules. The people had no voice in the way the country was governed. The delegates believed in the idea of majority rule, which means that a decision can be made only after the majority of people approve of it. The delegates did not want their new government to become too powerful, like a king. So they set up a government with separate powers for each branch.

An engraving of King George III of England. Experience with his tyrannical policies led the Founding Fathers to reject a monarchical form of government.

Paul Revere created this engraving of the four sides of the monument erected on Boston Common in celebration of the repeal of the Stamp Act in 1766. The inscriptions praise the wisdom of King George III, but soon the colonists would reject their loyalty to the British Crown.

There were some very new ideas in the Constitution. For the first time, individuals were given the right to elect their leaders. Another idea was the separation of church and state. This meant that there could not be an official religion that people would be forced to join. People were free to worship the way they pleased.

ARTICLE the THIRD.

Congrefs fhall make no law eftablifhing articles of faith, or a mode of worfhip, or prohibiting the free exercife of religion, or abridging the freedom of fpeech, or of the prefs, or the right of the people peaceably to affemble, and to petition to the government for a redrefs of grievances.

From the printed copy of the first draft of the Bill of Rights by James Madison, this article guaranteed separation of church and state, freedom of speech and of the press, and the right of assembly and petition. It was eventually made the First Amendment to the Constitution.

The original signed copy of the Constitution of the United States, completed in 1787 and ratified by the states in 1788.

The delegates intended the Constitution to last a long time. They knew that there might be a need for changes. So they agreed that there could be amendments, or additions, to the Constitution. On September 17, 1787, the final draft of the Constitution was signed by the delegates. Then it went to the states to be ratified, which took almost a year. On July 2, 1788, the necessary nine states had ratified the Constitution. It was now the law of the nation.

Did You Know?

The youngest signer of the Constitution was 26-year-old Jonathan Dayton. The oldest signer was 81-year-old Benjamin Franklin.

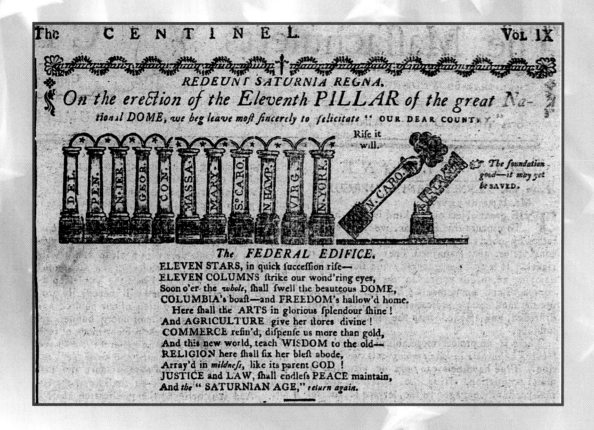

The CENTINEL.   VOL IX

REDEUNT SATURNIA REGNA.

On the erection of the Eleventh PILLAR of the great National DOME, we beg leave most sincerely to felicitate "OUR DEAR COUNTRY."

Rise it will.

DEL. PEN. N. JER. GEOR. CON. MASSA. MARY. S° CARO. N. HAMP. VIRG. N. YORK. N. CARO. RHODE ISLAND

☞ The foundation good—it may yet be SAVED.

The FEDERAL EDIFICE.

ELEVEN STARS, in quick succession rise—
ELEVEN COLUMNS strike our wond'ring eyes,
Soon o'er the *whole*, shall swell the beauteous DOME,
COLUMBIA's boast—and FREEDOM's hallow'd home.
  Here shall the ARTS in glorious splendour shine!
And AGRICULTURE give her stores divine!
COMMERCE refin'd; dispense us more than gold,
And this new world, teach WISDOM to the old—
RELIGION here shall fix her blest abode,
Array'd in *mildness*, like its parent GOD!
JUSTICE and LAW, shall endless PEACE maintain,
And *the* " SATURNIAN AGE," *return again.*

This drawing depicts the United States as a great dome supported by those states that quickly ratified the Constitution. North Carolina and Rhode Island, who withheld ratification for a time, are shown here as crumbling pillars threatening the stability of the nation.

When the Constitution was adopted in 1788, the delegates weren't quite finished. James Madison added the first ten amendments, known as the Bill of Rights, at the insistence of some of the delegates. They became law on December 15, 1791. The first eight amendments list the basic rights and freedoms of each citizen. The Ninth Amendment keeps the government from limiting any rights not listed in the Constitution. The Tenth Amendment limits the government's powers to those spelled out in the Constitution.

A portrait of George Mason, one of the Founding Fathers whose ideas deeply influenced Thomas Jefferson when he wrote the Declaration of Independence. Mason was also a major influence in the creation of the Bill of Rights.

The scene at Federal Hall, New York City, overlooking Wall and Broad Streets, where Washington was inaugurated president on April 29, 1789.

Delegate James Madison, who later became a president of the United States, said about the Constitution, "In framing a system which we wish to last for ages, we should not lose sight of the changes which ages will produce." Including the Bill of Rights, there have been only 27 amendments since 1787.

James Madison is known as the father of the Constitution. Along with Alexander Hamilton and John Jay, he co-authored the Federalist Papers. He became the fourth president of the United States.

The original draft of the first twelve amendments to the Constitution. Only ten of them were approved by Congress, and these ten amendments are known as the Bill of Rights.

Some of those amendments are very important. They have abolished slavery and extended civil liberties to African Americans and women. They have given the government the right to tax a citizen's income. They have forbidden anyone from holding the office of president for more than two terms.

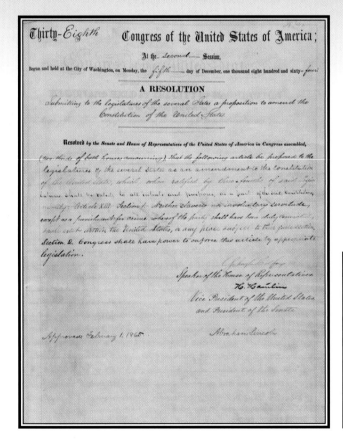

The Thirteenth Amendment to the Constitution, passed by Congress in 1865, abolished slavery in the United States.

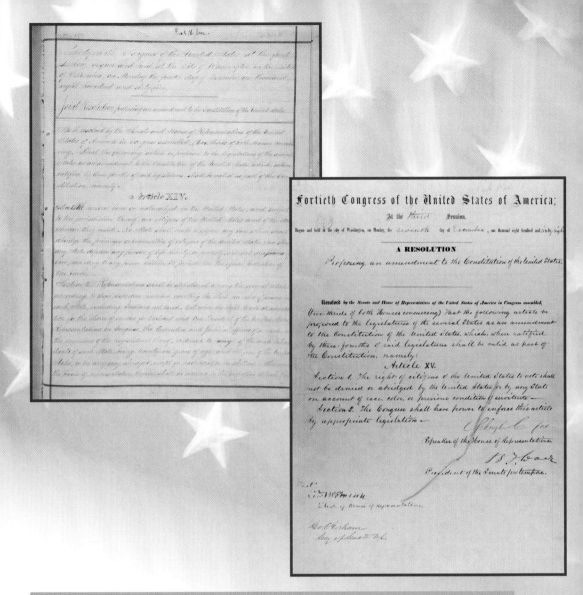

While the Thirteenth Amendment abolished slavery, the Fourteenth Amendment *(left)* was passed by Congress in 1866 and granted former slaves citizenship and equal protection under the law. The Fifteenth Amendment *(right)* was passed by Congress in 1870 and granted former slaves the right to vote.

The United States is one of the strongest countries in the world. Its government is one of the most stable governments. Yet it can adapt to changing circumstances and new political challenges. The creators of the United States Constitution did a magnificent job.

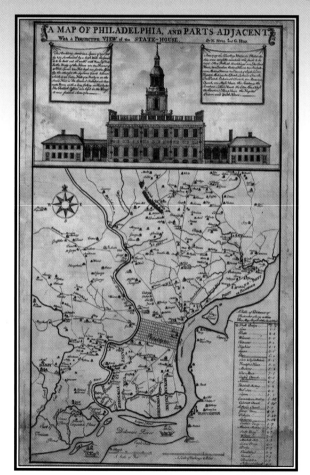

This early map of Philadelphia includes a picture of the Pennsylvania State House (Independence Hall).

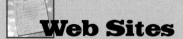

Glossary

amendment (ah-MEND-ment) The formal revision or changing of a document.

confederation (kon-fed-uh-RAY-shun) A group united for a common cause.

constitution (kon-sti-TOO-shun) The fundamental law or legal code of a country.

delegate (DEL-uh-gayt) A representative of a group who is sent to a conference or convention.

ratify (RA-ti-fi) To approve a law.

Web Sites

Due to the changing nature of Internet links, the Rosen Publishing Group, Inc., has developed an online list of Web sites related to the subject of this book. This site is updated regularly. Please use this link to access the list:

http://www.rosenlinks.com/pslac/cons

Primary Source Image List

Cover (left): *The Foundation of American Government,* painted by Henry Hintermeister, 1925, now with the Library of Congress.

Cover (top right) and page 4: *The Philadelphia State House*, engraved by Karl Bodmer in 1834.

Page 5: Assembly room, Independence Hall, photographed by Lester Lefkowitz, 2000.

Page 6: *British Retreat to Boston*, engraved by Amos Doolittle from first-hand accounts. Courtesy of the Massachusetts Historical Society.

Page 8: Roger Sherman, a 1780 engraving copying the painting by Alonzo Chappel (1828–1887).

Page 9: The Articles of Confederation, 1777, now with the National Archives.

Page 10: George Washington, painted by Gilbert Stuart (1755–1828).

Page 11: Alexander Hamilton's notes, 1787, now with the Library of Congress.

Page 12: *The Constitutional Convention, 1787,* engraved for *A History of the United States of America,* published by Huntington & Hopkins in 1823.

Page 13: Acts of Congress, 1789, now in the Manuscript Division of the Library of Congress.

Page 14: Charles C. Pinckney, engraved after a portrait by Alonzo Chappel (1828–1887).

Page 15: The Virginia Plan by James Madison and Edmund Randolph, now in the National Archives.

Page 16: Alexander Hamilton, engraved by Frederick Girsch.

Page 17: Oliver Ellsworth, painted by James Sharples, now with the Library of Congress.

Part 18: King George III, engraved in 1802 by Robert Harley, now with the Library of Congress.
Page 19: *Repeal of the Stamp Act*, engraved by Paul Revere in 1766, now with the Library of Congress.
Page 20: James Madison's Bill of Rights, now with the Library of Congress.
Page 21: Constitution of the United States, now with the National Archives.
Page 23: *The Federal Edifice*, a cartoon from the *Massachusetts Sentinel*, 1788.
Page 24: George Mason, an etching by Albert Rosenthal in 1888.
Page 26: A portrait of James Madison, painted by Charles Willson Peale (1741–1827).
Page 27: The Bill of Rights, 1791, now with the National Archives.
Page 28: The Thirteenth Amendment, 1865, now with the National Archives.
Page 29: The Fourteenth and Fifteenth Amendments to the Constitution, 1865 and 1870, now with the National Archives.
Page 30: *The Philadelphia State House (Independence Hall)*, by Nicholas Scull, 1752, now with the Library of Congress.

Index

About the Author

Josepha Sherman is a professional author and folklorist, with more than forty books and 125 short stories and articles in print. She is an active member of the Authors Guild.